Great Peace
for
Mothers

Other Books by Shirley D. Hicks

Great Peace for the Storms of Life

Great Peace for New Beginnings

Great Peace for Today

Great Peace for Women

Great Peace for Men

Great Peace for Ministers

Great Peace for Wives

Great Peace for Leaders

Great Peace for Using Your Gifts & Talents

and others…

A companion journal is available for each book in the series.

See all of the books and journals in the *Great Peace Series for Christian Living* at:

www.GreatPeace.com

Great Peace for Mothers

How to Find Peace in Difficult Times from Mothers in the Bible

SHIRLEY D. HICKS

Great Peace for Mothers

Copyright © 2017 by Shirley D. Hicks

ISBN 13: 978-1-947688-06-3

Great Peace Enterprises LLC
Alexandria, VA

www.GreatPeace.com

Dedicated
to every mother who needs
peace in a difficult time

CONTENTS

ACKNOWLEDGMENTS

I would like to thank my Lord and Savior, Jesus Christ, for giving me this book and the opportunity to share it with mothers everywhere.

I would also like to thank my husband, Chris, and my daughter, Christen, for their love, support, and help in writing this book.

In addition, I would like to thank my mother, Lillie M. Kelly, and my mother-in-law, Annie B. Hicks, for being two of the best mothers in the world.

Great peace have they which love thy law:
and nothing shall offend them.
Psalm 119:165

INTRODUCTION

Motherhood is a role that brings joys as well as challenges. Throughout the Bible, we find mothers who faced many of the same problems that mothers face today. We have the awesome privilege of seeing how God worked in their lives and how He gave them victory in their troubled times.

This book can help provide the godly strength that you may need in facing difficult situations as a mother. It contains ten themes that include some of the most common problems that mothers face. Each theme focuses on a particular mother in the Bible. It also includes a biblical insight, an inspirational poem, and scriptures that incorporate the theme in a powerful, but practical way. God has already provided in His Word everything you need for any problem that you may face as a mother. Look into the lives of mothers in the Bible and find the peace you need to endure the difficult times of motherhood.

www.GreatPeace.com

As a mother comforts her child,
so will I comfort you.
Isaiah 66:13 (NIV)

Bold Belief

~

Mary

Mary

And the angel said unto her, Fear not, Mary:
for thou hast found favour with God.
Luke 1:30

Who was Mary?
Mary was the mother of Jesus and the wife of Joseph.

Where is her Story?
Her story is in Matthew 1, Luke 1, Luke 2.

What problem did she face?
An angel appeared unto Mary and told her that she would have a son who would be the Messiah. At the time, she was not married, but was engaged to her future husband, Joseph.

How did God work in her life?
Mary believed the words that the angel said, but she was not yet married to Joseph. An angel also appeared unto Joseph and told him to take Mary as his wife, and he did. Mary had a son as the angel proclaimed, and Joseph named him Jesus. He is the Messiah, the Savior of the world.

5

Mary, the mother of Jesus, faced a difficult situation where belief was the key to what God was calling her to do. In Luke 1:46 Mary was filled with joy and gladness when the angel told her she would have a son who would become the Savior of the world.

Mary's situation seemed impossible because she was not even married or ever had any relationship with a man. However, she believed the angel in a seemingly impossible situation. In Luke 1:38, Mary said, "Be it unto me according to thy word." She had a son, just as the angel said.

If God tells you that He wants to do something in your life that seems impossible, what would your response be? Do you believe He is able to do whatever He is speaking to your heart today? God wants you to respond in faith when He tells you that He is going to do something great for you. Hebrews 11:6 says, "But without faith it is impossible to please him: for he that cometh to God must believe that he is, and that he is a rewarder of them that diligently seek him."

Believe God when He sends good news to you. No matter how impossible the situation may seem, Luke 1:37 tell us that, "with God nothing shall be impossible." Boldly reply in faith, "Be it unto me according to thy word."

Mary Shows Us…

Believe God even when we do not have all the answers.
Mary asked the angel, "How can these things be?" How could she understand something so divine, unusual, and extraordinary? Yet, she believed God's word even when she did not understand everything that was happening in her life.

Other people may not understand.
At first, Joseph did not understand what was happening in Mary's life. God, however, showed Joseph in a dream that He was working in Mary's life. Many other people probably did not understand either. Still, Mary and Joseph believed God, despite other people's misunderstandings.

God can bless you in an unconventional way.
God blessed Mary in a way that was divinely extraordinary. Mary experienced the joys and the burdens of God's blessings in an unconventional way. In it all, she faithfully said, "Be it unto me according to thy word."

And she shall bring forth a son,
and thou shalt call his name JESUS. Matthew 1:21

7

In Your Life…

Do you believe God when you do not have answers?
Like Mary, some things may come into your life that leaves you asking, "How can these things be?" When you do not understand God's way, you still must believe Him and know that He is always planning what is best for you.

Should you believe when other people question God?
When God is working in your life, find your direction and guidance from Him. Pray fervently and seek God's face so you can know His will for your life. Other people may not understand, but you must still believe.

Is God blessing you in an unconventional way?
Perhaps God is trying to do something unconventional in your life. Allow Him to bless you in a way that may be divinely extraordinary. You may experience the joys as well as the burdens of God's blessings in an unusual way, but you can believe God and say, "Be it unto me according to thy word."

Believe God.

Your Belief

And Mary said, Behold the handmaid of the Lord;
be it unto me according to thy word.
Luke 1:38

An angel told Mary she would have a son,
And she was God's special chosen one.
But Mary asked, "How can these things be?"
He said, "God's power will overshadow thee."
Then, Mary, responding to what she heard,
Said, "Be it unto me according to thy word."

~

Mary had faith and trusted God even more,
For something that never happened before.
She believed God and she didn't ask why,
But she trusted Him and gave a great reply.

~

If God speaks to you and makes a decree,
Do you know what your response would be?
Would you respond to Him in fear and dread,
Or say, "Let it be just as you have said."

~

If He wants to use you to do something great,

9

Believe Him and do not make the mistake,
Of not trusting Him to do something new,
But trust Him to do great things in you.

~

You can have faith and trust God even more,
For something that never happened before.
Believe His word and do not ask why,
But trust Him and give Him a great reply.

~

He wants to use you to do something great,
Believe Him and do not make the mistake,
Of not trusting Him to do something new,
But trust Him to do great things in you.

****

Promises for Belief

Behold, I set before you this day a blessing and a curse; A blessing, if ye obey the commandments of the LORD your God, which I command you this day.

Deuteronomy 11:26-28

Behold, to obey is better than sacrifice, and to hearken than the fat of rams.

1 Samuel 15:22

Then Peter and the other apostles answered and said, We ought to obey God rather than men.

Acts 5:29

But this thing commanded I them, saying, Obey my voice, and I will be your God, and ye shall be my people: and walk ye in all the ways that I have commanded you, that it may be well unto you.

Jeremiah 7:23

So obey the commands of the LORD.

Deuteronomy 8:6(NLT)

If ye keep my commandments, ye shall abide in my love; even as I have kept my Father's commandments, and abide in his love.

John 15:10

Therefore everyone who hears these words of mine and puts them into practice is like a wise man who built his house on the rock. The rain came down, the streams rose, and the winds blew and beat against that house; yet it did not fall, because it had its foundation on the rock.

Matthew 7:24-25 (NIV)

See, I have set before thee this day life and good, and death and evil; In that I command thee this day to love the LORD thy God, to walk in his ways, and to keep his commandments and his statutes and his judgments, that thou mayest live and multiply: and the LORD thy God shall bless thee in the land whither thou goest to possess it.

Deuteronomy 30:15-16

And we will receive from him whatever we ask because we obey him and do the things that please him.

1 John 3:22 (NLT)

If God speaks to you and makes a decree,
Do you know what your response would be?

Fortified Faith

~

The Canaanite Woman

The Canaanite Woman

*A Gentile woman who lived there came to him,
pleading, "Have mercy on me, O Lord, Son of
David! For my daughter is possessed by a demon
that torments her severely."*
Matthew 15:22 (NLT)

Who was the Canaanite Woman?

The Canaanite woman was the Gentile mother of a girl who lived in the region of Tyre and Sidon.

Where is her Story?

Her story is in Matthew 15:21-28, and Mark 7:24-30.

What problem did she face?

The Canaanite woman had a daughter who was demon-possessed.

How did God work in her life?

When the Canaanite woman approached Jesus with her request, He did not answer her right away. His ministry was to the Jewish people. However, when He saw her great faith, Jesus answered her and healed her daughter. Her faith helped to bring about a great miracle.

The Canaanite woman faced a difficult situation where faith was the key to her child's deliverance. Her daughter was possessed with a demonic spirit and she sought Jesus for her healing. As Jesus traveled through the region of Tyre and Sidon, she approached Him and asked Him to heal her daughter.

Jesus did not answer the woman because His ministry was to the Jewish people and she was a Gentile. Several times when she cried after Him, He ignored her. His disciples just wanted to send her away. After all, not only was she a woman, but also a Gentile, and the Jews had no dealings with the Gentiles.

The Canaanite woman was persistent in her request for her daughter's healing. She did not give up, even when Jesus did not answer her. She knew that the miracle she needed was in His hands, and she was not going to miss the opportunity to change her child's life forever. She fortified her faith even more. Jesus heard her cry and healed her daughter.

As a mother, you must be persistent in your request to God for your children. Do not miss the opportunity to pray for them, encourage them, and tell them about the love and faithfulness of God. Your faith can make the difference in your child's life forever.

The Canaanite Woman Shows Us...

God is listening.
At first, Jesus did not answer the Canaanite woman as she cried after Him. When He finally addressed her, He spoke rather harshly to her. This would have been enough to discourage most people, but not this desperate, unwavering mother. She knew that Jesus was finally listening to her cry.

With faith, all things are possible.
No racial, cultural, or social barriers can prevent God's blessings. Hebrews 11:6 says, "But without faith it is impossible to please him." Her faith in God superseded the social prejudices and stigmas of that day.

A mother must be persistent in prayer for her child.
The woman did not give up when Jesus ignored her. Perhaps her feelings were hurt, but it did not change the fact that she needed a miracle. She paid no attention to her feelings at that point. She persevered in faith, Jesus heard her cry, and healed her daughter.

And when she arrived home, she found her little girl lying quietly in bed, and the demon was gone. Mark 7:30 (NLT)

In Your Life…

Is God really listening to your prayers?
As you pray fervently for your child, remember that God's ears are open to your cry. Like the Shunammite woman, be persistent in your prayers. Believe that God will answer your prayers in His way.

Is deliverance really possible?
If you are facing racial, cultural, or social barriers, they are no match for God. In Matthew 19:26 (NIV), Jesus said, "With man this is impossible, but with God all things are possible." Have faith in God and pray for your deliverance, no matter how many obstacles seem to stand in your way.

Should you ever stop praying for your child?
Do not give up when you feel low. Your deliverance will not happen according to your feeling, but according to your faith. Persevere in simple, determined faith like the Canaanite woman, regardless of how you feel or how things may look.

**God will acknowledge and bless
your simple, determined faith.**

Simple Determined Faith

But without faith it is impossible to please him: for he
that cometh to God must believe that he is, and that
he is a rewarder of them that diligently seek him.
Hebrews 11:6

A Canaanite woman heard of Jesus one day,
She heard that He was passing her way,
She had a child who was demon-possessed,
And although she had tried her best,
To heal her daughter and set her free,
All efforts had failed miserably.

~

She saw Jesus, not as a man,
But as God with deliverance in His hands.
She cried after Him and called out His name,
But He did not answer, much to her shame.

~

She called after Him and continued to pray,
Until the disciples wanted to send her away.
But again and again she humbly cried,
Until Jesus finally replied.

~

And Jesus, being the God that He was,

Turned aside to help her because,
He was not moved by her status or race,
But by her simple, determined faith.

~

His words to her were harsh and few,
He said, "I have not been sent unto you."
She was a Gentile and this was contrary,
To His purpose. It was extraordinary,
Yet, she humbly came and fell at His feet,
And desperately cried, "Lord help me!"

~

Then Jesus, in love, firmly said,
"The dogs must not eat the children's bread."
Perhaps she was not worthy, this was true,
But there at His feet, what could she do?
As a Gentile outcast, a societal scum,
She cried, "Lord, the dogs eat of the crumbs!"

~

Then Jesus, filled with compassion and grace,
Said, "O woman, how great is your faith,
Be it unto you even as you will!"
But then His disciples were very still,
For with these people, they had no dealing,
Yet, Jesus was giving her daughter healing.
But the love of God is tender and kind,

It crosses all racial and cultural lines,
And He was not moved by her status or race,
But just by her simple, determined faith!

~

A determined faith, a determined mind,
Is faith that leaves all doubts behind,
And comes to God with every plea,
And prays and prays unceasingly.
That's faith of heavenly dimensions,
That's faith that captures God's attention.

~

It's faith that can move the mountains,
And open up Heaven's fountains,
Where God's great blessings are released,
It's faith in which God is well pleased.

~

For the love of God is tender and kind,
It crosses all racial and cultural lines,
And He is not moved by our status or race,
But just by our simple, determined faith.

****

Promises for Faith

And this is the victory that overcometh the world, even our faith.

I John 5:4

So then faith cometh by hearing, and hearing by the word of God.

Romans 10:17

The just shall live by faith.

Romans 1:17

For we walk by faith, not by sight.

II Corinthians 5:7

For verily I say unto you, If ye have faith as a grain of mustard seed, ye shall say unto this mountain, Remove hence to yonder place, and it shall remove, and nothing shall be impossible unto you.

Matthew 17:20

And Jesus answering saith unto them, Have faith in God.

Mark 11:22

Now faith is the substance of things hoped
for, the evidence of things not seen.

Hebrews 11:1

So then faith cometh by hearing, and hearing
by the word of God.

Romans 10:17

If any of you lack wisdom, let him ask of
God, that giveth to all men liberally, and
upbraideth not; and it shall be given him. But
let him ask in faith, nothing wavering. For he
that wavereth is like a wave of the sea driven
with the wind and tossed.

James 1:5-6

Therefore, since we are surrounded by such a
huge crowd of witnesses to the life of faith, let
us strip off every weight that slows us down,
especially the sin that so easily trips us up.
And let us run with endurance the race God
has set before us.

Hebrews 12:1 (NLT)

For by grace are ye saved through faith; and
that not of yourselves: it is the gift of God.

Ephesians 2:8

The love of God is tender and kind,
It crosses all racial and cultural lines.

Genuine Generosity

~

The Shunammite Woman

The Shunammite Woman

One day Elisha went to the town of Shunem. A wealthy woman lived there, and she urged him to come to her home for a meal. After that, whenever he passed that way, he would stop there for something to eat.
2 Kings 4:8 (NLT)

Who was the Shunammite woman?
The Shunammite woman was the mother of the boy that the prophet, Elisha, told her she would have miraculously.

Where is her Story?
Her story is in 2 Kings 4:8-37.

What problem did she face?
The Shunammite woman was wealthy, but she and her husband did not have any children.

How did God work in her life?
The Shunammite woman and her husband were very hospitable to Elisha. Because of their generosity, Elisha prophesied that she would have a son, and she did. Some years later, the boy died suddenly. She ran to Elisha in despair and he came to her home and miraculously raised her son from the dead.

The Shunammite woman faced a difficult situation where her generosity was the key to her deliverance. Although she was a wealthy woman, she was childless. She and her husband showed kindness to the prophet, Elisha. They built him a special room to stay in when he traveled through their land.

Elisha called her to him one day and told her that she would have a son. She replied to Elisha in 2 Kings 4:16 (NLT), "O man of God, don't deceive me and get my hopes up like that." Elisha's prophecy, however, came true and she had a son the following year.

Some years later, the boy died suddenly, but she rushed to Elisha and he miraculously revived him. Because of her generosity, God graciously blessed her twice - in giving her a son, and in raising him from the dead.

In a mother's life, giving is an important part of receiving. In Luke 6:38, Jesus said, "Give, and it shall be given unto you; good measure, pressed down, and shaken together, and running over, shall men give into your bosom." When you genuinely give your resources to God's work, He will bless you and give you things that you need for your family. Only God can give you some things, especially those things that money cannot buy.

The Shunammite Woman Shows Us…

God will bless you when you are a blessing to others.
Perhaps the Shunammite woman had wanted a child for so many years that it did not seem possible anymore. Nevertheless, when she and her husband were a blessing to Elisha, God miraculously blessed them with a son. Their miracle child was a direct result of their generosity to the man of God.

God can give you the things that money cannot buy.
Although she was wealthy, only God could have given her the thing that she deeply desired. She became a mother because of a miracle from God, and she received her son alive again because of a miracle from God.

You must not give up.
The Shunammite mother had already seen God do the impossible in blessing her with a son, so she did not give up when it appeared to be the end of his life. Instead, she rushed to Elisha for help. She learned that nothing is really over until God says it is over.

But the woman became pregnant, and the next year about that same time she gave birth to a son, just as Elisha had told her.
2 Kings 4:17 (NIV)

28

In Your Life…

Can you be a blessing to God's Kingdom?
Can you think of some ways that you can give
to the work of the Lord? Your giving will be
an important part of receiving the things that
you want from God. When you give to God's
work, He will bless you and your family.

What are some things that you desire?
You may need or desire something that
money cannot buy. Only God knows about
the secret desires of your heart, and the things
you really want as a mother. Be generous in
giving God your time, money, talents, and
other resources. Then watch Him give you the
things money cannot buy.

Will you believe God in impossible situations?
At some time or another in your life, you will
face a seemingly impossible situation as a
mother. Like the Shunammite woman, do not
give up, but believe that God is able to do the
impossible. Regardless of how things may
look for your child, it is not over until God
says it is over.

Believe that it's not over yet.

It's Not Over Yet

Now unto him that is able to do exceeding abundantly
above all that we ask or think,
according to the power that worketh in us.
Ephesians 3:20

If your plans fail and you don't know why,
No need to give up in despair and cry,
No need to worry and begin to fret,
But believe that it's not over yet.

~

When you suddenly reach a fork in the road,
And you feel like you're carrying a heavy load,
And the goals have failed that you once set,
Believe that it's not over yet.

~

Victory may take a little more time,
But don't let trouble fill your mind,
Despite how difficult things may get,
Believe that it's not over yet.

~

Write a new plan, create new goals,
Read the Bible and encourage your soul.
Revise the objectives that were not met,

And believe that it's not over yet.

~

It's not over until God brings you out,
And gives you favor that you can't doubt,
And delivers you and sets you free,
And gives your life true victory.

~

Just stand still because you can cope,
Fill your heart with faith and hope,
And make no decisions that you'll regret,
But believe that it's not over yet.

~

Your difficult time can't last always,
Prepare to see some brighter days.
God will come through, so never forget,
That it's not really over yet.

~

Yes, victory may take a little more time,
But please don't worry, you'll be fine.
Your day of deliverance is already set,
So believe that it's not over yet.

****

Promises for Generosity

Give, and you will receive. Your gift will return to you in full—pressed down, shaken together to make room for more, running over, and poured into your lap. The amount you give will determine the amount you get back.

Luke 6:38 (NLT)

Delight thyself also in the LORD; and he shall give thee the desires of thine heart.

Psalms 37:4

But seek first his kingdom and his righteousness, and all these things will be given to you as well.

Matthew 6:33 (NIV)

Honor the LORD with your wealth and with the best part of everything you produce.

Proverbs 3:9 (NLT)

But when you give to the needy, do not let your left hand know what your right hand is doing, so that your giving may be in secret.

Matthew 6:3-4 (NIV)

"Bring all the tithes into the storehouse so there will be enough food in my Temple. If you do," says the LORD of Heaven's Armies, "I will open the windows of heaven for you. I will pour out a blessing so great you won't have enough room to take it in! Try it! Put me to the test!"

Malachi 3:10 (NLT)

Ye ought to... remember the words of the Lord Jesus, how he said, It is more blessed to give than to receive.

Acts 20:35

Every man according as he purposeth in his heart, so let him give; not grudgingly, or of necessity: for God loveth a cheerful giver.

2 Corinthians 9:7

If you help the poor, you are lending to the LORD— and he will repay you!

Proverbs 19:17 (NLT)

And God will generously provide all you need. Then you will always have everything you need and plenty left over to share with others.

2 Corinthians 9:8 (NLT)

No need to worry and begin to fret,

But believe that it's not over yet.

Heartfelt Hope

~

Rahab

Rahab

Only Rahab the harlot shall live,
she and all that are with her in the house,
because she hid the messengers that we sent.
Joshua 6:17

Who was Rahab?
Rahab was the mother of Boaz, great-great-grandmother of King David, and ancestress of Jesus Christ.

Where is her Story?
Her story is in Joshua 2:1-21 and Joshua 6:17.

What problem did she face?
Rahab was a harlot in Jericho, a city that Joshua and the Israeli army were planning to destroy. Her future looked very bleak.

How did God work in her life?
Rahab hid the men that Joshua sent to spy out the city of Jericho when the King of Jericho was trying to capture them. Because of her kindness, Joshua spared her family when the Israelites destroyed the city. She later married Salmon and had a son named Boaz. Through her lineage, King David and Jesus were born.

Rahab faced a difficult situation where hope was the key to her deliverance. She was a notorious harlot who lived in the city of Jericho. In an effort to conquer the Promise Land, Joshua sent two spies into the city of Jericho. When the King of Jericho realized the spies were in the city, he sent a search party to find them. Rahab hid the spies and protected them from the impending danger.

Rahab's bold deed caused the Israelites to spare her family when they destroyed Jericho. It also led to a new beginning, which gave her new hope for her life. After the invasion, she was no longer a notorious harlot. She became the wife of an Israelite man named Salmon, and the mother of a son named Boaz.

Rahab became a great mother of the Bible and an ancestor of many famous men. Boaz, the rich ruler who married Ruth, was her son. King David was her great-great grandson. Historically, Rahab was a mother who blessed many generations because Jesus was also one of her descendants. Rahab's life demonstrates that God can bring you out of a difficult situation and make you a mother who will bless generations. He can put new hope in your heart, and bless you to do great things as a mother, and for the Kingdom of God.

Rahab Shows Us...

God can use whoever He wants to use.
How could God use someone with such an immoral character as Rahab? Rahab's life shows us that God's love, grace, and mercy are great. He will reach beyond our shortcomings and touch our lives in powerful and loving ways.

You must not be afraid to trust God for deliverance.
Rahab had to be bold to protect the spies from the King of Jericho, but her wise actions led to her deliverance. She became a great mother of the Bible because she was not afraid to trust God and help the Israelites.

God can give you new hope.
We do not know about Rahab's background, but we know that she was in a shameful situation when the spies met her. Yet, it was not so bad that God could not turn her life around and give her new hope. Rahab left a life of harlotry and God gave her new hope, a new life, and a blessed family.

By faith the prostitute Rahab, because she welcomed the spies,
was not killed with those who were disobedient.
Hebrews 11:31 (NIV)

In Your Life…

Can God use you?

You should not feel insufficient, dishonored, or inadequate for whatever God is calling you to do as a mother. God can use you for His glory. You may be in a bad situation because of wrong choices, or because of situations that were not your fault. In either case, turn to God and let Him give you new hope.

Are you afraid to trust God for deliverance?

If God calls you to a certain task, do it in faith, not fear. You may not know all the ways He will use you, but you must boldly believe that, "God hath not given us the spirit of fear; but of power, love, and a sound mind."

Do you have hope in your heart?

Even if you make mistakes, the grace and mercy of God can change your life and give you a divine destiny. God gave Rahab new hope and a new dream for her life. Despite your past, God can also give you new hope and a new dream for your life.

**With your hope and God's help,
you can dream again.**

A Broken Dream

He healeth the broken in heart,
and bindeth up their wounds.
Psalm 147:3

Put thou my tears into thy bottle:
are they not in thy book?
Psalm 56:8

I had a dream so sure,
It was precious from the start.
It was vivid in my mind
It was planted in my heart.

~

But then one day it faltered
And everything went wrong.
I was brokenhearted,
And my precious dream was gone.

~

I gathered all my heart
And hurried to God's throne.
Then He said to me,
"My child, what is wrong?"

~

As I searched for the words,

As I really tried to pray,
With my broken heart before Him,
This was all that I could say:
~

A broken dream, a broken heart,
Everything is all apart,
And my eyes are filled with tears,
And my heart is filled with fears.
~

He gently said to me,
"This is not the end,
Give Me your broken heart,
Let Me fix it back again."
~

He collected all my tears,
And as I quietly looked,
He put them in a bottle,
And wrote them in a book.
~

He healed my broken heart,
And much to my surprise,
He picked me up with love,
And looked into my eyes,
~

And gently said, "Don't be afraid,
This is not the end,
You're more than a conqueror,
So you must dream again!"
Then I got up from my knees,
Feeling confident and strong,
With my broken heart mended,
And a peace to go on.

~

And I thought to myself,
About what He said to me,
And I wondered still in my heart,
Could it really be?

~

Jesus took all my heartache,
And He took all my pain,
And He gently said to me,
That I must dream again.

~

So I'm trusting in His words,
Knowing this is not the end,
Because He fixed my broken heart,
And I know I must dream again.

****

Promises for Hope

Be of good courage, and he shall strengthen your heart, all ye that hope in the LORD.

Psalm 31:24

Let us hold tightly without wavering to the hope we affirm, for God can be trusted to keep his promise.

Hebrews 10:23 (NLT)

Now faith is the substance of things hoped for, the evidence of things not seen.

Hebrews 11:1

I say to myself, "The LORD is my inheritance; therefore, I will hope in him!"

Lamentations 3:24 (NLT)

May integrity and uprightness protect me, because my hope, LORD, is in you.

Psalm 25:21 (NIV)

My soul fainteth for thy salvation: but I hope in thy word.

Psalm 119:81

43

And Joshua saved Rahab the harlot alive, and her father's household, and all that she had; and she dwelleth in Israel even unto this day; because she hid the messengers, which Joshua sent to spy out Jericho.

Joshua 6:25

Likewise also was not Rahab the harlot justified by works, when she had received the messengers, and had sent them out another way?

James 2:25

Fear not; for thou shalt not be ashamed: neither be thou confounded; for thou shalt not be put to shame: for thou shalt forget the shame of thy youth, and shalt not remember the reproach of thy widowhood any more.

Isaiah 54:4

For your shame ye shall have double; and for confusion they shall rejoice in their portion: therefore in their land they shall possess the double: everlasting joy shall be unto them.

Isaiah 61:7

I will put my hope in God.

Psalm 42:5 (NLT)

Don't be afraid, this is not the end,
You're more than a conqueror,
so dream again!

Lofty Longing

~

Sarah

Sarah

Now Sarai Abram's wife bare him no children:
and she had an handmaid, an Egyptian,
whose name was Hagar.

Who was Sarah?
Sarah was the wife of Abraham and the mother of Isaac.

Where is her Story?
Her story is in Genesis 11 – Genesis 25.

What problem did she face?
Sarah did not have any children after being married for many years. She grew impatient and tried to solve the problem on her own.

How did God work in her life?
God promised Abraham that his wife, Sarah, would have a son. After waiting on God for many years, Sarah grew impatient and decided that Abraham should have a child with her handmaid. This terrible mistake caused much heartache and pain for everyone involved. Eventually, God blessed Sarah to have a son in spite of their mistake. Isaac, the promised child, was born in God's time.

Sarah faced a difficult situation where her longing for a child required God's deliverance. God appeared unto Sarah's husband, Abraham, in a vision and told him that his descendants would be as numerous as the stars in the sky. However, Sarah did not have a child, and she and her husband were very old. In her longing, Sarah decided that Abraham should have a child with her handmaid. That proved to be a big mistake.

Sarah waited many years, went through much heartache, and made mistakes as she waited for the Lord to give her a child. Yet, God, in His own time, did exactly what He promised. Sarah and Abraham finally had a son and they named him Isaac. While God blessed Sarah with a son, she still had to deal with the consequences of the mistake she made because she did not wait on God.

God understands the longing that a mother has in her heart, but He has His own timing and plans for answering your prayers. Waiting on God may not always be easy, but He knows what is best for you. When you trust His timing, He will help you avoid costly mistakes and give you what is best for the longing that you have in your heart.

Sarah Shows Us…

God's plans are often better than our plans.
Even when she faced a seemingly impossible situation, Sarah should have believed that God was able to do what He has promised. Perhaps she wrestled with fear, doubt, and unbelief, but God said in Isaiah 49:23, "They shall not be ashamed that wait for me."

Our decisions can affect other people's lives.
Sarah's recommendation to Abraham to have a child with her Egyptian slave, Hagar, affected her family, Hagar's family, and nations of people for many centuries afterwards. Sarah underestimated the harsh consequences of doing things her way.

Carefully consider the longing in your heart.
Sarah made a desperate decision that did not fill the longing in her heart, but caused even greater pain. It seemed to be a good idea at the time, but later proved to be a mistake. Waiting on God and His timing is always best.

It was by faith that even Sarah was able to have a child, though she was barren and was too old. Hebrews 11:11 (NLT)

In Your Life…

Do you trust God's plan?
Has God told you that He is going to bless you in some way? If so, can you wait for Him to bring it to pass? If you are facing big obstacles and seemingly impossible situations, do not get discouraged, but wait on God's timing and trust His plan for your life.

What major decisions are you making today?
If you have a major decision to make today, you should precede it with much prayer. Only God knows what the real impact of your decision will be. You cannot see how it may affect your child today and future generations.

Are you feeling desperate?
If you feel desperate, take your longings to God and wait for Him to show you what to do. Sarah learned that feelings of desperation can lead to actions that do not resolve your longings, but often lead to greater pain. Maybe the longings in your heart will help you better understand the decisions Sarah made.

**Your longings may help you
Understand Sarah**

Understanding Sarah

And Sarai said unto Abram, Behold now, the
LORD hath restrained me from bearing:
I pray thee, go in unto my maid;
it may be that I may obtain children by her.
And Abram hearkened to the voice of Sarai.
Genesis 16:1-2

I understand Sarah, how she wanted a child,
And became very discouraged after a while.
I understand Sarah and how she laughed,
When things looked bleak on her behalf,
I understand her longing to hold a child,
Close to her bosom just for a while.

~

I understand the pain and heartache she felt,
And maybe her heart was about to melt,
When years went by and no child was born,
When years went by and all hope was gone.

~

I understand her, knowing what God said,
Trying to work out the details in her head,
Going to Hagar and Abraham too,

51

When it seemed like the only thing left to do.

~

Could she see God's purpose and His plan?
In all of her longing, could Sarah understand,
That in God's time, He would bring it to pass,
And give her the promised child at last?
For God had a set time to bring her out,
Of all of her longing, worries, and doubts.

~

In God's perfect timing, Isaac was born,
And in His perfect timing, she had a son.
And in His time, His purpose for me,
Will be fulfilled, and I do believe,
That God has a set time to bring me out,
Of all of my longing, worries, and doubts.

~

And just like Sarah, I must understand,
In all of my longings is God's perfect plan.

****

Promises for Longing

You know what I long for, Lord; you hear my every sigh.

Psalm 38:9 (NLT)

Hope deferred makes the heart sick, but a longing fulfilled is a tree of life.

Proverbs 13:12 (NIV)

For he satisfieth the longing soul, and filleth the hungry soul with goodness.

Psalm 107:9

But seek ye first the kingdom of God, and his righteousness; and all these things shall be added unto you.

Matthew 6:33

But they that wait upon the LORD shall renew their strength; they shall mount up with wings as eagles; they shall run, and not be weary; and they shall walk, and not faint.

Isaiah 40:31

For I have learned, in whatsoever state I am, therewith to be content.

Philippians 4:11

The Lord hath been mindful of us: he will bless us.

Jeremiah 17:14

For your kingdom is an everlasting kingdom. You rule throughout all generations. The LORD always keeps his promises; he is gracious in all he does.

Psalm 145:13 (NLT)

Don't worry about anything; instead, pray about everything. Tell God what you need, and thank him for all he has done. Then you will experience God's peace, which exceeds anything we can understand. His peace will guard your hearts and minds as you live in Christ Jesus.

Philippians 4:6-7 (NLT)

Give your burdens to the LORD, and he will take care of you. He will not permit the godly to slip and fall.

Psalm 55:22 (NLT)

Now the Lord of peace himself give you peace always by all means.

2 Thessalonians 3:16

Just like Sarah, I must understand,
In all of my longings is God's perfect plan.

Natural Need

~

The Widow

The Widow

One day the widow of a member of the group of prophets came to Elisha and cried out ... a creditor has come, threatening to take my two sons as slaves.
2 Kings 4:1 (NLT)

Who was the widow?

The widow was the mother of two sons whose deceased father had been a prophet that worked with Elisha.

Where is her story?

Her story is in 2 Kings 4:1-7.

What problem did she face?

The widow did not have any money to pay her bills and a creditor came to her, threatening to take her two sons as slaves.

How did God work in her life?

The widow only had a flask of oil in her house. Elisha told her to borrow as many jars as she could from her neighbors. God miraculously multiplied the oil so that she was able to fill every jar with oil. Then she sold the oil and was able to pay all of her creditors.

The widow faced a difficult situation where God's divine provision was the key to her deliverance. She was a woman whose husband had been a prophet in Elisha's group. She came to Elisha one day in a desperate situation. She had bills she could not pay and the creditors were threatening to take away her two sons as slaves.

Elisha asked the widow what she had in her house. She was so poor that she only had a flask of oil. To Elisha, she already had what she needed. He knew that God would take the little she had and multiply it to make it become whatever she needed.

Elisha told the widow to borrow as many jars as she could from her neighbors and fill them with the oil in the flask. Although it did not seem very logical, she followed his orders. Miraculously, God multiplied the oil until she was able to fill all of the jars with oil. She then sold the oil and paid her debts.

As a mother, you may also have a desperate need for your family. If so, what is in your house? Could it be that you already have something that God can use to fill your need? Consider your gifts, talents, and other assets. Ask God to show you how to use what you have to fulfill your need.

The Widow Shows Us…

God can provide for you in miraculous ways.
The widow was in a desperate situation where her children were about to be sold as slaves. Nevertheless, God gave her a miracle in the midst of her desperation. He provided just what she needed for her family in a miraculous way.

When you give to God, He will give back to you.
The widow's husband had been a member of the group of prophets. She reminded Elisha of how her husband served him faithfully and feared the Lord. Although her husband was no longer alive, God was still blessing his family because of his faithfulness.

God can multiply what you have in your house.
The widow thought she did not have anything worthy in her house. Yet, Elisha told her to use the little flask of oil that she had. When she used what she already had in her house, God multiplied it until it became what she really needed.

Then go into your house with your sons and shut the door behind you. Pour olive oil from your flask into the jars, setting each one aside when it is filled. 2 Kings 4:4 (NLT)

59

In Your Life…

Do you need a miracle today?
Are you anxious or worried about a need that you have in your family? God can give you a miracle in the midst of your problem, and He can provide just what you need. Ask Him to bless you.

Are you giving to God?
God will honor your faithfulness in giving to the Lord's work. In 2 Corinthians 9:7-8 (NIV), Paul wrote, "Each of you should give what you have decided in your heart to give, not reluctantly or under compulsion, for God loves a cheerful giver."

What do you have in your house?
You may feel as if you do not have anything worthy in your house to use. Ask God to show you what you already have in your house that He can multiply until it becomes what you really need.

**What you need may be
in your house.**

In the House

"What can I do to help you?" Elisha asked.
"Tell me, what do you have in the house?"
2 Kings 4:2 (NLT)

A widow came to Elisha one day,
When she had a big debt to pay.
She and her sons were very upset,
Because she could not pay the debt.

~

Yet, in her house, Elisha could see,
She already had what she would need,
To solve the problem and pay the debt,
In a way that she would never forget.

~

She had no money or help from a spouse,
But just a flask of oil in her house.
Although her problem looked very bad,
Elisha told her to use what she had.
He told her to gather many pots and pans,
And use the little she had in her hands.

~

She obeyed him and put her faith to the test,
She used what she had, and God did the rest.

61

She went in her house and shut the door,
And poured the oil until she had no more.

~

Then God took the little and multiplied it.
It was miracle and she couldn't deny it.
All of the pots and pans were filled,
Which gave her the means to pay her bills.

~

Then she sold the oil and paid her debt,
And all of her needs were miraculously met,
For God supplied all her needs,
When she trusted Him and believed.

~

What's in your house? Could it be,
That you must use your creativity,
And take what you have and give it your best,
Then God will step in and do the rest?

~

When you are at the end of your wits,
You cannot give up and you cannot quit.
Ask God to show you what to do,
He will provide and take care of you.

~

Don't feel sad and hold your head down,
But look to Jesus, then look all around.

Perhaps in your house, you have all you need,
To solve your problem if you only believe.

~

Ask God for an idea or a plan,
He knows your needs, He understands.
The little you have will become much,
When He blesses it with His divine touch.

~

Don't be discouraged, but believe,
You already have what you need
Take it now and give it your best,
Then God will step in and do the rest.

~

Go into your house and shut the door,
And pour until you have no more.
Pour out what God has given you,
For He will show you what to do.

~

Yes, God will bless and multiply,
The little you have so you can't deny,
That He will supply your every need,
When you trust Him and believe.

****

Promises for Need

But my God shall supply all your need according to his riches in glory by Christ Jesus.

Philippians 4:19

I will lift up mine eyes unto the hills, from whence cometh my help. My help cometh from the LORD, which made heaven and earth.

Psalm 121:1-2

I have been young, and now am old; yet have I not seen the righteous forsaken, nor his seed begging bread.

Psalm 37:25

He will rescue the poor when they cry to him; he will help the oppressed, who have no one to defend them. He feels pity for the weak and the needy, and he will rescue them.

Psalm 72:12-14 (NLT)

But I am poor and needy; yet the Lord thinketh upon me: thou art my help and my deliverer.

Psalm 40:17

For he shall deliver the needy when he crieth; the poor also, and him that hath no helper. He shall spare the poor and needy, and shall save the souls of the needy.

Psalm 72:12-13

The LORD is my shepherd; I shall not want.

Psalm 23:1

"So don't worry about these things, saying, 'What will we eat? What will we drink? What will we wear?' These things dominate the thoughts of unbelievers, but your heavenly Father already knows all your needs. Seek the Kingdom of God above all else, and live righteously, and he will give you everything you need."

Matthew 6:31-33 (NLT)

Take no thought for your life, what ye shall eat; neither for the body, what ye shall put on. The life is more than meat, and the body is more than raiment. Consider the ravens: for they neither sow nor reap; which neither have storehouse nor barn; and God feedeth them: how much more are ye better than the fowls?

Luke 12:22-24

In your house, you have all you need,
To solve your problem if you only believe.

Persistent Prayer

~

Hannah

Hannah

And she vowed a vow, and said, O LORD of hosts, if thou wilt… give unto thine handmaid a man child, then I will give him unto the LORD.
1 Samuel 1:11

Who was Hannah?
Hannah was the wife of Elkanah and the mother of Samuel.

Where is her Story?
Her story is in 1 Samuel 1-2.

What problem did she face?
Hannah did not have any children after being married to for many years. God blessed her with a son that she gave back to Him.

How did God work in her life?
Hannah prayed fervently for a son for many years and vowed to give him back to the Lord. The Lord answered her prayers and blessed her with a son whom she named Samuel. She gave Samuel back to the Lord as she promised and he became a great prophet, priest, and judge. Afterwards, God blessed Hannah with three more sons and two daughters.

Hannah faced a difficult situation where her prayers were the key to her deliverance. She did not have any children after being married to Elkanah for many years, and she felt discouraged and hopeless. In her difficult situation, she prayed to the Lord and asked Him to give her a son.

Hannah promised the Lord that she would give the child back to Him if He answered her prayers. God, through Eli, the priest, granted Hannah her request and blessed her with a son named Samuel. Hannah fulfilled her vow and gave Samuel back to the Lord and he became a great prophet, priest, and judge in Israel.

Prayer is a very powerful privilege that you have as a mother to present your problems to God. It is not God's will for you to worry or fret about situations. Jesus said in Luke 18:1 that we should always pray and not faint, or lose hope. No matter what your problem may be, He cares for you and your child. You have the awesome opportunity to come before the throne of God with the concerns of your life and conquer your worry with prayer. No problem is too hard for God. In fact, with God all things are possible. So keep praying for your child.

Hannah Shows Us…

Prayer works.
Hannah was in bitterness of soul and prayed unto the Lord, and wept, but she did not give up on God's ability to answer her prayer. She knew the power was in His hands to bless her, even after praying for many years.

We must pay the vows we make to God.
Hannah did not receive the child from God and then forget about what she promised Him. She was faithful to pay her vow. Surely, it was a difficult thing to do, but she did it willingly. Because of her faithfulness, God blessed her with five more children.

God can use our children at a young age.
Samuel was very young when Hannah left him with Eli at the temple, and he was a blessing to the ministry. In 1 Samuel 2:11, the child "did minister unto the Lord before Eli the priest." Also, 1 Samuel 2:26 says, "And the child Samuel grew on, and was in favor both with the Lord, and also with men."

For this child I prayed; and the LORD hath given me my petition which I asked of him. 1 Samuel 1:27

In Your Life…

Can prayer work in your situation?
Are you discouraged and burdened about something that is happening in your life? If so, do not give up on God's ability to answer your prayers, even if you have been praying for many years. God has the power in His hands to bless you. Keep praying.

Have you made any promises to God?
When we really want God to answer our prayer, we may promise to do something big for Him. If you made a promise to God, do what you promised Him and be faithful to your vow.

Do you see ways in which God can use your child?
Even when our children are young, they can be a blessing to the ministry. Ask the Lord to show you how you can instill the things of God into the heart and mind of your child at a young age so that he or she will be "in favor both with the Lord, and also with men."

**God will bless a child
when a mother prays.**

When a Mother Prays

And all thy children shall be taught of the LORD;
and great shall be the peace of thy children.
Isaiah 54:13

Sometimes as a mother, we all know it's true,
That you may not know exactly what to do,
But trust in God's grace and merciful ways,
He will answer prayers when a mother prays.

~

When the child that you love is feeling down,
Or Satan has your child terribly bound,
Or if your child is living in spiritual decay,
God will step in when a mother prays.

~

Do not let the problems burden you down,
Only God can turn some things around.
Bend on your knees for your child every day,
And tell God about it and sincerely pray.

~

To the throne of grace, you must run,
And pray for your daughter or for your son,
And tell the Lord the problems they face,
Ask Him for His mercy and His grace.

Regardless of what your child has done,
Pray for your daughter or for your son,
Believe that God's help is on the way
When you kneel and sincerely pray.

~

When you pour out your heart and distress,
And stay at God's feet until He says "Yes"
God will move in miraculous ways,
When a loving mother sincerely prays.

~

You must pray and keep holding on,
And believe that it will not be long,
Before God removes the trouble and strife,
And divinely touches your child's life.

~

Pray that your child's life will be blessed,
Ask God to please send Heaven's best.
Then watch Him move in amazing ways,
When you give Him your child and pray.

~

A mother's love will always be strong,
So stand in faith and keep holding on.
Bend on your knees for your child every day,
Just tell God about it and sincerely pray.

****

73

Promises for Prayer

Ask, and it shall be given you; seek, and ye shall find; knock, and it shall be opened unto you.

Matthew 7:7

And we are confident that he hears us whenever we ask for anything that pleases him.

1 John 5:14 (NLT)

Then Jesus told his disciples a parable to show them that they should always pray and not give up.

Luke 18:1 (NIV)

But when you pray, go away by yourself, shut the door behind you, and pray to your Father in private. Then your Father, who sees everything, will reward you.

Matthew 6:6 (NLT)

Pray without ceasing.

1 Thessalonians 5:17

For the eyes of the Lord are over the righteous, and his ears are open unto their prayers: but the face of the Lord is against them that do evil.

1 Peter 3:12

And this is the confidence that we have in him, that, if we ask any thing according to his will, he heareth us: And if we know that he hear us, whatsoever we ask, we know that we have the petitions that we desired of him.

1 John 5:14-15

You parents—if your children ask for a loaf of bread, do you give them a stone instead? Or if they ask for a fish, do you give them a snake? Of course not! So if you sinful people know how to give good gifts to your children, how much more will your heavenly Father give good gifts to those who ask him.

Matthew 7:9-11 (NLT)

Behold, the LORD'S hand is not shortened, that it cannot save; neither his ear heavy, that it cannot hear:

Isaiah 59:1

Pray that your child's life will be blessed,
Ask God to please send Heaven's best.

Supernatural
Success

~

Elizabeth

Elizabeth

*And, behold, thy cousin Elisabeth, she hath also
conceived a son in her old age: and this is the sixth
month with her, who was called barren.*
Luke 1:36

Who was Elizabeth?
Elizabeth was the mother of John the Baptist
and the wife of Zechariah the priest.

Where is her Story?
Her story is in Luke 1.

What problem did she face?
Elizabeth did not have any children after
being married for many years. God eventually
blessed her with a special child.

How did God work in her life?
Elizabeth and Zechariah were an elderly
couple who devoutly served God, but they did
not have any children. An angel appeared to
Zechariah and told him that they would have
a son whose name would be John. God
miraculously blessed them with a son in their
old age as the angel said. Their son, John,
became the forerunner for Jesus Christ.

Elizabeth faced a difficult situation where her success could only come from the hand of God. She had been married to the priest, Zachariah, for many years, but they did not have any children. They were old and the possibility of ever having a child seemed hopeless. Yet, God showed them that He still had the power to give them success.

An angel appeared unto Zachariah one day in the temple and told him that they would have a child. Zachariah couldn't believe it. However, it happened just as the angel said. After Elizabeth became pregnant, she hid herself for six months. Perhaps she wanted to make sure it was really going to happen. Perhaps she felt ashamed because she was so old. God, however, gave her success in spite of how she felt. Elizabeth had a son who became the forerunner of Jesus Christ.

Are you facing some type of barren situation today? You may be experiencing a very difficult problem that makes you think there is no hope for success. God, however, can give you supernatural success in your barren places. Your success can come from the hand of God. Luke 1:37 says, "For with God nothing shall be impossible." Don't give up now, but look to Jesus for your success.

Elizabeth Shows Us...

It is never too late for God to work.
When Elizabeth's prayers were not answered, when the situation seems hopeless, even when they had given up in despair, God blessed them. He knows how to give you victory over what seems to be defeat.

You cannot hide when God gives you success.
After Elizabeth realized that she was pregnant, she isolated herself for five months. Eventually, she came out of hiding and everyone knew of her blessing. God wanted to receive the glory from her success so others would know of His love, mercy, and power.

Love and serve God in a barren situation.
Elizabeth had been barren for many years, but neither she nor Zechariah allowed that situation to keep them from serving God devoutly. Zechariah was diligently serving in the temple when the angel approached him with the news.

But the angel said unto him, Fear not, Zacharias: for thy prayer is heard; and thy wife Elisabeth shall bear thee a son, and thou shalt call his name John. Luke 1:13

In Your Life…

Do you think it is too late for God to work?
If God has not answered your prayers and your situation seems hopeless, trust Him for what He wants to do in your life. God knows how to bless you in any circumstance, and give you victory over what seems to be defeat.

Are you hiding your successes?
Has God done something special for you that you have not told anyone else about? God does not want you to hide your blessings. He wants to receive the glory from your successes so others may know of His love, mercy, and power.

Will you love and serve God in a barren situation?
God may not answer all of your prayers as you think He should. He may not work out all of your situations in the way that you desire. Nevertheless, you should serve him in spite of your barrenness and believe that He will ultimately bless you in wonderful ways.

**God can give you success
over your barrenness.**

Your Barrenness

I will open rivers in high places, and fountains in the midst of the valleys: I will make the wilderness a pool of water, and the dry land springs of water.
Isaiah 41:18

Of all the things a woman faces,
One of the hardest is barren places,
The times in life that are parched and dry,
And often leave you wondering why,
Why has God forgotten me?
Doesn't He understand and see,
That barrenness is like a stronghold,
That brings much pain to a woman's soul?

~

Yet, many women in the Bible were blessed,
After years of suffering barrenness,
And saw God do amazing things,
With the barrenness that life can bring.
If some of those women were here today,
These are the things that I would say:

~

I would take Sarah by the hand,
And say, "I know, I understand.

82

Some read your story and are confused,
But they never walked in your shoes.
Although it took quite a while,
God gave you Isaac, the promised child."

~

To Rebekah, I would widely grin,
And say, "God blessed you with the twins.
And your grandchildren became twelve tribes,
That the nation of Israel now subscribes,
As their ancestors and lineage too.
Isn't it amazing what God can do?"

~

And to Rachel, I would surely say,
"God blessed Joseph in an awesome way.
He faced great trials, but he survived,
And helped to keep many people alive."

~

If Manoah's wife ever came along,
I'd say, "Your son, Samson, was very strong.
Perhaps he didn't do everything right,
But in the end, he won the fight."

~

If I could see Hannah, I would say,
"You really showed me how to pray.
Your son, Samuel, was a prophet so true,

Isn't it amazing what God can do?"

~

To the Shunammite women who was so nice,
I'd say, "God really blessed you twice.
He gave you a son as Elijah said,
Then later raised him from the dead."

~

Finally, I would look Elizabeth in her eyes,
And say, "God gave you quite a surprise,
When you had a child much later in life,
But John became the forerunner for Christ."

~

The barrenness that each woman tasted,
Was not forgotten and was not wasted.
So continue to do the best that you can,
And place your barrenness in God's hands.

~

Only God can take what seems unfair,
The big disappointments and pain you bear,
And place you safely under His wings,
And bring about some amazing things.

~

So be encouraged and be blessed,
God wants to give you good success,
He has a plan designed for you,

No matter what you are going through.

~

Your barrenness is not a waste,
For He is God of the barren place,
And He is God of the hot, dry ground.
He can turn your problems all around.

~

God can make rivers in desolate places,
For the barrenness that a woman faces.
He said, in the desert, He will make a stream,
No matter how barren your life may seem.

~

He can make dry land springs of water,
So don't be discouraged today, my daughter.
In whatever barrenness you go through,
Just watch and see what God will do.

****

Promises for Success

He maketh the barren woman to keep house, and to be a joyful mother of children. Praise ye the LORD.

Psalm 113:9

He holds success in store for the upright, he is a shield to those whose walk is blameless.

Proverbs 2:7 (NIV)

The LORD will guide you always; he will satisfy your needs in a sun-scorched land and will strengthen your frame. You will be like a well-watered garden, like a spring whose waters never fail.

Isaiah 58:11 (NIV)

He will ensure my safety and success.

2 Samuel 23:5 (NLT)

Study this Book of Instruction continually. Meditate on it day and night so you will be sure to obey everything written in it. Only then will you prosper and succeed in all you do.

Joshua 1:8 (NLT)

Remember the LORD your God. He is the one who gives you power to be successful.

Deuteronomy 8:18 (NLT)

For the LORD God is a sun and shield: the LORD will give grace and glory: no good thing will he withhold from them that walk uprightly.

Psalm 84:11

Then you will have success if you are careful to observe the decrees and laws that the LORD gave Moses for Israel. Be strong and courageous. Do not be afraid or discouraged.

1 Chronicles 22:13 (NIV)

I answered them by saying, "The God of heaven will give us success."

Nehemiah 2:20 (NIV)

Commit thy way unto the LORD; trust also in him; and he shall bring it to pass.

Psalm 37:5

He holds success in store for the upright, he is a shield to those whose walk is blameless.

Proverbs 2:6-7 (NIV)

In the desert, He will make a stream,

No matter how barren your life may seem.

Transforming
Trouble

~

Ruth

Ruth

*But Ruth replied, "Don't urge me to leave you or to
turn back from you. Where you go I will go, and
where you stay I will stay. Your people will be my
people and your God my God."*
Ruth 1:16 (NIV)

Who was Ruth?

Ruth was the mother of Obed, grandmother
of Jesse, great-grandmother of King David,
and ancestress of Jesus Christ.

Where is her Story?

Her story is in the Book of Ruth.

What problem did she face?

Ruth was a young, impoverished widow who
traveled to Bethlehem from Moab with her
mother-in-law, Naomi.

How did God work in her life?

Ruth married one of Naomi's wealthy
relatives named Boaz. Afterwards, she was no
longer a poor widow, but an affluent wife.
God brought about events in her life that
changed the world. Through her lineage, King
David and Jesus Christ were born.

Ruth and her mother-in-law, Naomi, faced a difficult situation that God used to transform their lives. Because of a famine in Bethlehem, Naomi and her husband, Elimelech, had migrated to Moab along with their two sons. In Moab, the two sons married Moabite women, one of which was Ruth. Later, all three men of the family died and Ruth and Naomi returned to Bethlehem discouraged, poor, and destitute.

In Ruth 1:20 when Naomi arrived in Bethlehem, she told the people not to call her Naomi, which means almighty, but to call her Mara, which means bitterness. She told them that the almighty had made her life very bitter. Little did she know that Ruth would marry a wealthy man named Boaz, and through this lineage, Jesus Christ would be born. In the midst of their trouble, God had a plan to bless Ruth and Naomi and generations to come.

Trouble is inevitable in life. Jesus said in John 16:33 (NIV), "In this world you will have trouble. But take heart! I have overcome the world." In spite of the trouble, God has a plan to bless you. Allow Him to use your difficult situation to transform your life. When you trust Him, He can use your trouble to bless you and, perhaps, generations to come.

Ruth Shows Us…

You will experience some trouble.
As children of God, Naomi and Ruth encountered trouble that left them empty, broken, and bruised. But God did not leave them in a desolate state. He ultimately blessed their lives in ways that they could have never imagined. Although Naomi tasted the bitterness of life, it was only for a season.

What didn't work in the past may work in the future.
Ruth had been married before to Naomi's son, Mahlon, but they had no children. However, in her new marriage to Boaz, God blessed her to have a son named Obed. She not only became a mother, but also a matriarch of King David and the Messiah.

God is able to turn your trouble completely around.
Although Ruth was a foreigner, Boaz, a very wealthy man, willingly married her. Perhaps it was not difficult for him because his own mother, Rahab, was a foreigner from Jericho.

So Boaz took Ruth, and she was his wife.
Ruth 4:13

In Your Life...

Are you experiencing trouble today?
As a mother, you will encounter trouble in life that may leave you empty, broken, and bruised. God promised to be a place where you can go for divine comfort. Psalm 9:9 says, "The Lord also will be a refuge for the oppressed, a refuge in times of trouble."

Is God doing a new thing in you?
Look into your past and see if you can find something that did not work before, but it might be possible now. Perhaps God wants to do a new thing in your life that will bless you, your child, and many generations to come.

God is able to turn your trouble completely around.
Although trouble is inevitable, it cannot last always. It is only for a season. In God's time, and in God's way, He will turn your trouble completely around and richly bless your life. Be strong in the Lord and in the power of His might until the storm passes over. Soon God will give you brighter tomorrows.

**God can give you
brighter tomorrows.**

Brighter Tomorrows

"Don't call me Naomi," she responded.
"Instead, call me Mara,
for the Almighty has made life very bitter for me."
Ruth 1:20 (NLT)

Naomi felt as if her life was cursed,
As her problems grew from bad to worse,
When her husband and her two sons died,
She began to feel broken and bitter inside.

~

She thought, "God, tell me, how could it be,
That many bad things have happened to me?
I've lost my husband and my sons,
What is it, Lord, that I have done?"

~

Now Ruth was all she had left,
So she began to feel sorry for herself.
How could she go on and happily live,
A life where she had no more to give?

~

As she wrestled with the pain and the sorrow,
She told everyone to call her Mara,
For Mara means bitter and that's how she felt,

She didn't understand the hand she was dealt.

~

But God can take your pain and sorrow,
And exchange them for brighter tomorrows.
And that's what He did for Naomi and Ruth,
Both of their lives displayed this truth,
That we may experience hurt and pain,
But God knows how to bless us again,
And give us a life that He lovingly fills,
According to His purpose and holy will.

~

God blessed them both and sent a man,
Who married Ruth and fulfilled God's plan.
For she had a son in the fullness of time,
And the Messiah was born in their family line.
Through Naomi and Ruth's hurt and scorn,
Jesus Christ, the Savior, was born.

~

So, trust the Lord and give Him your sorrows,
Then He will give you a brighter tomorrow.
For only God can take your hurt and pain,
And wonderfully bless your life again.

****

Promises for Trouble

God is our refuge and strength, a very present help in trouble.

Psalm 46:1

Though I walk in the midst of trouble, thou wilt revive me.

Psalm 138:7

And my people shall be satisfied with my goodness, saith the LORD.

Jeremiah 31:14

Be of good courage, and he shall strengthen your heart, all ye that hope in the LORD.

Psalm 31:24

For the LORD will not forsake his people for his great name's sake: because it hath pleased the LORD to make you his people.

1 Samuel 12:22

I will not leave you comfortless: I will come to you.

John 14:18

But the salvation of the righteous is of the LORD: he is their strength in the time of trouble.

Psalm 37:39

The LORD is good, a strong hold in the day of trouble; and he knoweth them that trust in him.

Nahum 1:7

I have told you all this so that you may have peace in me. Here on earth you will have many trials and sorrows. But take heart, because I have overcome the world.

John 16:33 (NLT)

Rejoice not against me, O mine enemy: when I fall, I shall arise; when I sit in darkness, the LORD shall be a light unto me.

Micah 7:8

The LORD is my rock, and my fortress, and my deliverer; my God, my strength, in whom I will trust; my buckler, and the horn of my salvation, and my high tower. I will call upon the LORD, who is worthy to be praised: so shall I be saved from mine enemies.

Psalm 18:1-3

We may experience hurt and pain,
But God knows how to bless us again.

Tremendous
Trust

~

Hagar

Hagar

And God heard the voice of the lad; and the angel of God called to Hagar out of heaven, and said unto her, What aileth thee, Hagar? fear not; for God hath heard the voice of the lad where he is.
Genesis 21:17

Who was Hagar?
Hagar was the mother of Ishmael, Abraham's first son.

Where is her story?
Her story is in Genesis 16 and Genesis 21.

What problem did she face?
Because of family problems, Abraham sent Hagar and Ishmael away from his home and they wandered in the wilderness of Beersheba with no food, water, or shelter.

How did God work in her life?
When Hagar and Ishmael were on the brink of death in the wilderness, God sent an angel to help them. He gave them the things they needed as they trusted in him. Eventually, Ishmael grew up and became the father of a great nation, just as God promised he would.

Hagar faced a difficult situation where trusting God was the key to her deliverance. As a single mother, she had nowhere to turn when Abraham and Sarah expelled her out of their home because Ishmael was mocking their son, Isaac. Hagar's situation was the direct result of someone else's mistake. How could she provide for her son now in the dangerous, arduous wilderness of Beersheba with no food, water, or shelter?

God, however, did not forget about Hagar and Ishmael. He had already promised to bless them. He used the difficult time in the wilderness to prepare Hagar for a new life in a world where she would have to trust in Him to survive. God sent an angel to help them, and He continued to bless them as Ishmael grew up. Ishmael became the father of a great nation, as God promised he would.

Like Hagar, you may find yourself in an unexpected situation that leaves you and your child nearly destitute. God, however, will not leave you. He understands your situation completely and He is ready and willing to help you. God not only has plans for your life, but He will bless your child also. Trust Him to guide you and provide for you and your family in the tough times.

Hagar Shows Us…

God sees when a mother is mistreated.
Hagar's difficult situation was a consequence of Sarah's idea for her to have a child from Abraham. As an Egyptian slave, she had no say in the matter, and she suffered mistreatment in many ways because of it. Yet, each time, God blessed her in spite of the abusive situation she had to endure.

God will bless a mother with the support she needs.
When Hagar had nowhere to go and no one to turn to for help, God sent her help in a miraculous way. He said in Isaiah 54:5 (NLT), "For your Creator will be your husband." God can take care of a mother when she puts her trust in Him.

God has a plan for your child.
Although Abraham forsook Ishmael, God promised to bless him. He said to Hagar in Genesis 17:20, "I will make him a great nation." In Hagar's destitution and heartache, God already had a plan to bless them greatly.

And God was with the lad; and he grew, and dwelt in the wilderness, and became an archer. Genesis 21:20

In Your Life…

Are you in an abusive situation?
Your difficult situation may be a direct consequence of someone else's actions where you really had no say in the matter. If you are suffering mistreatment in any way, ask God to help you. He sent an angel to help Hagar, and He can send someone to help you.

Do you need support?
If you have nowhere to go and no one to turn to for help, ask God to send you help in a miraculous way. As a child of God Almighty, you can boldly approach the throne of grace and cast your cares upon Him. He will help you when you put your trust in Him.

What about your child?
God has a plan for your child's life even if a father has forsaken him or her. As in Ishmael's life, perhaps God is planning to bless your child in an amazing way and do great things in his or her life. Keep praying for your child and trust God. He will not forget about you.

God will be a husband to you.

Your Maker

*For thy Maker is thine husband; the LORD of hosts
is his name; and thy Redeemer the Holy One of Israel;
The God of the whole earth shall he be called.*

Isaiah 54:5

When there was no husband in Hagar's life,

God said He would take her as His wife,

And he would not leave or forsake her,

He said, "Your husband will be your Maker"

~

She only had God and no other,

For she had become a single mother.

It was not any fault of her own,

But God said He wouldn't leave her alone.

~

He calmed her fears and her frustrations,

And she became the mother of a nation.

He gave her everything she needed,

And despite her problems, she succeeded.

Only God can love and cherish you,
When times are hard and friends are few,
When others tend to leave you out,
He will calm your fears and your doubts.

~

He will be with you through thick and thin,
He will be with you until the end,
And care for you all of your days,
And bless your child in remarkable ways.

~

Don't be discouraged, but understand,
No one can love you like God can.
No matter what you are going through,
Your God will take good care of you.

****

Promises for Trust

And they that know thy name will put their trust in thee: for thou, LORD, hast not forsaken them that seek thee.

Psalm 9:10

When my father and my mother forsake me, then the LORD will take me up. *Psalm 27:10*

Trust in the LORD with all thine heart; and lean not unto thine own understanding.

Proverbs 3:5

The LORD hath been mindful of us: he will bless us.

Psalm 115:12

He raiseth up the poor out of the dust, and lifteth up the beggar from the dunghill, to set them among princes, and to make them inherit the throne of glory.

1 Samuel 2:8

Trust in him at all times; ye people, pour out your heart before him: God is a refuge for us.

Psalm 62:8

Trust in the LORD with all thine heart; and lean not unto thine own understanding. In all thy ways acknowledge him, and he shall direct thy paths.

Proverbs 3:5-6

Trust in the LORD, and do good; so shalt thou dwell in the land, and verily thou shalt be fed. Delight thyself also in the LORD; and he shall give thee the desires of thine heart. Commit thy way unto the LORD; trust also in him; and he shall bring it to pass.

Psalm 37:3-5

But rather seek ye the kingdom of God; and all these things shall be added unto you. Fear not, little flock; for it is your Father's good pleasure to give you the kingdom.

Luke 12:31-32

Many will see what he has done and be amazed. They will put their trust in the LORD. Oh, the joys of those who trust the LORD, who have no confidence in the proud or in those who worship idols.

Psalm 40:3-4 (NLT)

Don't be discouraged, but understand,

No one can love you like God can.

Yielding
Your Life

~

You

You

For it is God who works in you.
Philippians 2:13 (NIV)

Who are you?

What is your story?

What problems do you face?

How is God working in your life?

You may be facing a difficult situation today where you need God to work in your life. This book has given you the opportunity to look into the lives of some of the mothers in the Bible and see how God worked in their lives. But the story is not over. God also wants to work in your life. He is ready, willing, and able to help you in whatever difficult situation you may be facing as a mother today.

Despite what you may be going through, God can give you success in your troubles when you trust Him and give Him your life. Yield your life to the plan and purpose that He has for you. When you do, He will bless you and make you a blessing. Then your life will be a story that you can share with others. Just like the mothers you've read about in this book, you will have a story to tell.

You can show us...

How God worked in your life.
Every mother will have difficulties and challenges in life. Although each mother's experiences are unique, your testimony can be a source of inspiration and encouragement to mother who are experiencing difficult situations. Share your testimony so other mothers can be motivated to trust God in their difficult situations.

How you used your gifts and talents for God.
God has given you gifts and talents that are uniquely and genuinely yours. You can use them to bless the Kingdom of God in a way that no one else can.

How your life blessed others.
Whether through your life, your testimonies, your gifts, or your service, you can be a blessing to mothers. As you walk with God, He will receive glory from your life and you will be a godly example for mothers who are following in your footsteps.

Live so God can get the glory,
Live and tell others your story.

Tell Your Story

Let the redeemed of the LORD tell their story—
those he redeemed from the hand of the foe,
Psalm 107:2 (NIV)

The Word of God is faithful and true,
It's a book that was written just for you.
But the Bible is not where the story ends.
For in every life, God will begin,
To reveal himself and show you,
How He can work in your life too.
~

Hear His voice and heed His call,
And give to Him your all and all,
And live so God can have the glory,
Yes, live so you can share your story.
~

Write your story down on pages,
That others can read through the ages,
And see the things that you went through,
And how God worked them out for you.

****

Promises for You

Tell your children about it in the years to come, and let your children tell their children. Pass the story down from generation to generation.

Joel 1:3 (NLT)

Everyone will share the story of your wonderful goodness; they will sing with joy about your righteousness.

Psalm 145:7 (NLT)

This shall be written for the generation to come: and the people which shall be created shall praise the LORD.

Psalm 102:18

One generation shall praise thy works to another, and shall declare thy mighty acts.

Psalm 145:4

Let me proclaim your power to this new generation, your mighty miracles to all who come after me.

Psalm 71:18 (NLT)

Don't you realize that in a race everyone runs, but only one person gets the prize? So run to win!

1 Corinthians 9:24 (NLT)

But this one thing I do, forgetting those things which are behind, and reaching forth unto those things which are before, I press toward the mark for the prize of the high calling of God in Christ Jesus.

Philippians 3:13-14

But seek ye first the kingdom of God, and his righteousness; and all these things shall be added unto you.

Matthew 6:33

Look, I am coming soon! My reward is with me, and I will give to each person according to what they have done. I am the Alpha and the Omega, the First and the Last, the Beginning and the End.

Revelation 22:12-13 (NIV)

As long as it is day, we must do the works of him who sent me. Night is coming, when no one can work.

John 9:4 (NIV)

Write your story down on pages,
That others can read through the ages.

The Great Peace Series
for Christian Living

Finding Great Peace in the Word of God

The books in the *Great Peace Series for Christian Living* venture into the pages of the Bible and explore the lives of people just like you. In these books, you will learn how people with real problems experienced God in a real way during the difficult times of life. Each book includes biblical insights and inspirational poetry, as well as many pages of promises from the Word of God. Together, the Bible people, poetry, and promises will help you find the great peace that only God can give.

The Great Peace Series for Christian Living includes books for enduring the storms of life, beginning again, and facing each new day. The series also includes books written specifically for women, men, mothers, fathers, wives, husbands, parents, ministers, leaders, and more. Each book in the series has a companion journal that you can use to capture your personal thoughts and notes. Discover how you can find great peace in the Word of God through this series of inspirational books at www.GreatPeace.com.

ABOUT SHIRLEY D. HICKS

Shirley D. Hicks is a writer of Christian inspirational books and poetry. Her books in the *Great Peace Series for Christian Living* are a source of encouragement for people who are facing difficult and challenging times. After spending several years reading and studying the Bible, Shirley decided to pursue her passion for writing Christian books. Her writings have inspired and blessed many people. With Bachelor of Science degrees in Computer Science and Math, Shirley spent more than fifteen years as an IT professional. She also has a Master of Art degree in Theological Studies from Liberty University, Lynchburg, Virginia. She and her husband have one daughter. Visit her website at www.GreatPeace.com.

*Get the companion **Journal** to this book!*

The *Great Peace for Mothers Journal* includes encouraging excerpts from the *Great Peace for Mothers* book, plus one hundred pages for your journal entries. Get a copy today and write your story!

Great Peace
for
MOTHERS
Journal

How to Find Peace in Difficult Times
from Mothers in the Bible

The Great Peace for Mothers
JOURNAL

Be Inspired by Women in the Bible!

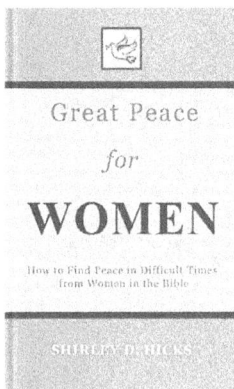

See all of the books in the

Great Peace Series for Christian Living

at

www.GreatPeace.com

www.ingramcontent.com/pod-product-compliance
Lightning Source LLC
Chambersburg PA
CBHW051043030426
42339CB00006B/167